P9-EMG-910

QUIET STRENGTH

MEN'S BIBLE STUDY

Discovering God's Game Plan for a Winning Life

Group

LOVELAND, COLORADO

Credits
Contributors: Tony Dungy, Karl Leuthauser
Project Manager: Scott M. Kinner
Editor: Scott M. Kinner
Copy Editor: Ann Jahns
Senior Developer: Roxanne Wieman
Chief Creative Officer: Joani Schultz
Art Director: Jeff Storm
Book Designer: The DesignWorks Group
Cover Art Designer: The DesignWorks Group
Print Production Artist: The DesignWorks Group
Production Manager: DeAnne Lear

ISBN 978-0-7644-3662-8
10 9 8 7 6 5   16 15 14 13 12 11 10 09 08 07

Printed in the United States of America.

CONTENTS

FOREWORD

The total weight of an average National Football League team of 53 players is over 13,000 pounds. It can take a lot of work to get that 6 ½ tons moving in the same direction—the right direction. It has always been a theme in my career to help move an NFL team in the *right* direction in a Christ-like way. There are many ways to coach a team of professional athletes. But I've always believed that God wants me to model certain principles and make serving Him my purpose—as a father, as a husband, on the field, or on the sideline.

As I wrote my memoir *Quiet Strength*, six guiding principles from my life emerged. I wanted to share these six principles with men, like you, who desire to grow in true strength:

> ❷ *What is your game plan?* When I was fired from Tampa Bay, I knew that my game plan needed to change. I had planned to be there much longer than I was. And I knew a change would be difficult for my family. But God's plans were different, and I quickly learned the importance of following God's plan—and glorifying Him no matter where I am. This section of the Bible study will challenge you to find God in the midst of frustrated plans.

> ❷ *What is strength?* When I played for the Pittsburgh Steelers in the 70s, I joined a group of Christian teammates who studied the Bible together. One of the passages we studied focused on

Nehemiah and his strength. I think this set the tone for my growth in Christ. It certainly taught me a valuable lesson about what strength is—and isn't. The lessons from Nehemiah were also constantly exemplified by my father. He showed me how to stay focused and make a difference in the face of adversity. He taught me that real strength isn't a steely lack of sensitivity and obnoxious ranting; it's humble and gentle leadership. This section of the study will use Nehemiah's example to help you focus on the source of your truest strength.

❯ *What is success?* At one point in my life, I thought being drafted as a quarterback into the NFL would surely be a sign of success. I was never drafted. In fact, nobody even wanted me as a quarterback. There went my vision of success. I still played, though in a different position. I had to reevaluate what success really meant to me: using my God-given talents, gifts, and abilities to serve and glorify Him in whatever position I'm in. This section will challenge you to define success in your own terms…beyond what you do.

❯ *What is your security?* It's easy for a professional athlete to place his security in influence, money, and ability. But all those things of this life can be pulled from you instantly. That's certainly what I experienced when I lost my son in 2005. Real security is in far greater things, though. It's in everything I know to be true: the love of my family in all parts of life, the joy of Christ's embrace when other things are stripped away, and the secure promise of eternal life with no pain or tears. This session will help you build a foundation that is truly secure.

● *What is your significance?* I learned early in my career that if I put my significance in football, I'd be disappointed many times a season...even winning seasons. Instead, my significance is in who I am as a husband, a father, and a child of God seeking to bring him glory. One of my coaches many years ago reminded me that football is what I'm doing *now*. I need to always prepare myself for my true life's work—serving God. Let this section challenge you to find your significance in making a difference in other people and bringing God glory.

● *What is your legacy?* Everything we do adds an element to the story we'll leave behind. My father left a legacy that I desire to pass on to my children. My legacy isn't what I say or do on the football field. It's what I say and do when people don't see me. It's about being faithful to God in the work He's given me. In this section, my charge to you is this: really evaluate your legacy, then seek to build that story you'll leave behind.

My life isn't about football. It's about glorifying God wherever He has me. This Bible study isn't about football, either. It's about the principles and priorities that have guided my life—and that I hope will guide yours. My prayer is that this study will open your heart to discover God's plan to make your life a winning life.

—Tony Dungy

INTRODUCTION

Before winning Super Bowl XLI, before leading two different NFL teams to winning records, even before playing for the Pittsburgh Steelers, Tony Dungy made a decision: to live his life with *Quiet Strength*—the way God intended. This Bible study takes an in-depth look at the winning principles, practices, and priorities from the life of Tony Dungy, head coach of the Super Bowl XLI champions the Indianapolis Colts, and applies them to your life.

The questions you'll explore in this study are six questions men often ask of themselves throughout their lives. They're questions Coach Dungy addresses in his memoir *Quiet Strength*. You'll discover the principles that come from these questions over the next six weeks.

Here's how this study works:

First, the study is meant to be done in a group setting—it could be a men's breakfast on Saturday morning, a small group meeting in a home or a restaurant, or even a lunch group at work. Everyone in your group will participate in discovering the principles of a winning life.

You'll also want to make sure everyone gets a copy of this book. We recommend each guy having a copy of Tony Dungy's

Quiet Strength, too. We'll refer to his book in several optional activities.

Briefly, here's how the sessions break down.

THINK ABOUT IT

This time will be spent thinking about the question for the session. A simple experience will help you walk through your thoughts on the topic, then you'll talk about the connections you made to your life.

TALK ABOUT IT

During this section, you'll take the question for the session a little deeper. The discussion here will tie your life connections to the Bible passages in the next section. This is an important time to get to know other guys' hearts and walk with each other through this discovery.

STUDY IT

This section will challenge you as you dig into God's Word. It's a time where you can see the principles you discover exemplified in the Bible. You'll connect your discussion and experiences from before to your discoveries in different passages through further discussion and sharing.

LIVE IT

This brings the study full circle. Just as you started the session reflecting on your life, you'll have a chance to reflect again as you connect what you've taken from the study to your life. The activities will guide you in making these connections.

COMMIT TO IT

Before you conclude your session, it's important to commit to an action point that will help you continue to grow. We'll give you three options to choose from.

WHAT IS YOUR GAME PLAN?

Finding God in the Midst of Frustrated Plans

WHAT EACH PERSON WILL NEED:

> Bible

> Pen

> His driver's license or photo ID

> *Quiet Strength: Men's Bible Study* guide

THINK ABOUT IT *(20 minutes)*

To get this session started, and to get to know each other a little more, allow each person to share a dream he had when he was in high school. For example, you may have dreamt of being an actor or that you would one day marry the head cheerleader. If men in your group are still in high school, have them share dreams they had when they were in grade school. If some of your group members haven't met, make sure you each share your name and the reason you came to this group.

 No decent coach plans to have a losing season. Even the coaches who see talent gaps on their teams strive to

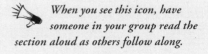 *When you see this icon, have someone in your group read the section aloud as others follow along.*

overcome the odds to lead their teams to the Big Game. In the NFL, 32 coaches start the season with a plan to win the Super Bowl, and 31 of them fail—every year.

Before leading the Indianapolis Colts to a Super Bowl championship following the 2006 season, Tony Dungy had his share of failed plans. His 2001 season as head coach for the Tampa Bay Buccaneers wasn't exactly a losing season. In fact, they made it to the playoffs. And that's when they lost and became one of the 31. So when Coach Dungy was fired after the stinging playoff loss following that season, he knew God's plans were different than his own. For all he could tell, his NFL career was over.

Is life turning out like you hoped it would? Are things going according to your game plan? Or maybe you've never created a specific plan or goal for your life; you just had a vague idea of where you'd like to be at this time in your life. For each of the areas on the next page, take a moment to jot down some thoughts about where you are in life and how that compares to where you thought you'd be. This table is just between you, God, and this book—so be honest. Take five to 10 minutes to go through this inventory.

Life Area	What I Planned	Where I Am
Career/school		
Family		
Skills/education/experience		
Finances		
Friends/relationships		
Faith/ministry		

TALK ABOUT IT

(10 minutes)

 Maybe a few things on the right side of your chart are a little disappointing to you...or maybe—hopefully—some of the items in the right column have actually turned out better than you planned. For better or worse, it's highly likely that many of the events and ideas about your life haven't worked out exactly according to plan.

Imagine that your life thus far is one football season of 10 games. The plan was

"It was hard to figure. My family had come to Tampa for a reason. God had led us here, opened doors that we didn't expect would be open, and allowed us to connect deeply with this community. But for what purpose?

"Not football, apparently. I felt certain that the Buccaneers were my best, and possibly last, chance to lead an NFL team. For whatever reason, God had closed the door. For what?"

—*Tony Dungy*
Quiet Strength

to win all 10 games, but how would you say you're really doing? What is your life "record" right now? Maybe you have a happy family, a safe home, and some frustrations at work. You could say your current record is 8-2. Share and explain your record with everyone in the group.

When everyone has finished, discuss:

❯ HOW HAVE YOUR PLANS FOR LIFE BEEN INTERRUPTED OR THWARTED?

❯ HOW HAS LIFE TURNED OUT BETTER THAN EXPECTED?

❯ READ PROVERBS 16:3 AND 9. HOW HAVE YOU SEEN GOD'S HAND IN BRINGING YOU TO WHERE YOU ARE TODAY?

❯ DO YOU THINK GOD WOULD GIVE YOU THE SAME "RECORD" YOU GAVE YOURSELF? WHY OR WHY NOT?

USELESS TRIVIA

You probably know that the current NFL regular season lasts 16 games. In the 1920s professional teams didn't have set schedules and could play as few as eight games. The NFL has had a 16-game regular season schedule since 1978. Which two years since 1978 have seen fewer than 16 games in the regular season and why? (See page 71 for the answer.)

STUDY IT *(15 minutes)*

In an episode of the show Blue Collar TV, comedian Jeff Foxworthy joked that every guy was "almost" a professional athlete in some sport. Injuries, angry coaches, or the lack of desire stopped them. There are hundreds of thousands of high school football players who dream of playing in the NFL and only 1,696 active positions in the NFL in any season. Only a very select few will realize their plan to play professional sports. We can make our plans, but the Lord determines our steps. Let's look at a man in the Bible who had a drastic change in plans.

Read Acts 9:1-19. Discuss:

❯ WHAT DO YOU THINK SAUL WAS THINKING AND FEELING WHEN VERSES 5-6 AND 9 TOOK PLACE? EXPLAIN.

❯ COMPARE AND CONTRAST SAUL'S PLAN IN VERSES 1-2 WITH GOD'S PLAN IN VERSES 15-16. WHAT DOES YOUR COMPARISON SUGGEST ABOUT HOW GOD WORKS IN OUR LIVES?

❯ HOW HAS GOD INTERRUPTED YOUR GAME PLAN FOR LIFE? WHAT GOOD HAS COME OR MAY COME FROM THAT INTERRUPTION?

❯ HOW CAN THAT KNOWLEDGE HELP YOU WHEN YOU ENCOUNTER FUTURE INTERRUPTIONS?

USEFUL TRIVIA

The Bible doesn't say that God changed Saul's name to "Paul." Why did Saul's name change to "Paul" starting with Acts 13? (See page 71 for the answer.)

LIVE IT *(15 minutes)*

In his book Quiet Strength, *Coach Dungy says, "God had already selected the team I would be coaching. I just needed to do my current job well, keep preparing, and wait on God's timing. I needed to trust His leadership, rather than try to force an outcome I wanted." You may have dreams to move to a different city, to change jobs, to launch a ministry, or to change things in your family. It's important to chase those dreams. It's just as important to understand where God has you* right now *and to find what God wants you to do* right where He has you. *Your life and ministry start* right now.

Get in groups of two to four. Pull out your driver's license. Take a look at the date it was issued. Discuss how your life has changed since that date.

Take a look at the expiration date. Discuss what you hope happens in your life by that date.

Take a look at your picture. Discuss how you can best serve God where He has you *right now* in life.

❷ READ EPHESIANS 2:10. WHAT DO YOU THINK GOD WANTS YOU TO DO TODAY? THIS MONTH? THIS YEAR?

❷ HOW ARE YOU GOING TO GET STARTED?

Put all of the driver's licenses facedown in the middle of the table. Each person should pick up one license. Pray together that God will help you bounce back from frustrated plans and move forward with plans He has for you now. Each person should pray for the person whose license he picked up.

COMMIT TO IT

Before you conclude this session, choose to complete one of the action points that follow or another action point you come up with. Commit to completing the action point before your next meeting, and be prepared to share what happened or what you learned.

OPTION 1: Read chapters 1-3 of Tony Dungy's *Quiet Strength*. Highlight or underline each example where life didn't go exactly as Coach Dungy had planned.

OPTION 2: It's easy to get frustrated when we look at how life hasn't gone according to our game plan. It's important to remember that God's plan for you is better than any plan you dream up. Read Jeremiah 29:11, then make a list at the bottom of this page of all the things you're grateful for.

OPTION 3: Find out how you're really doing by asking the people you impact. Follow the example in this session's Talk About It section on page 15 to find your "record" in the following areas:

> ❯ ASK YOUR SPOUSE WHAT YOUR RECORD WOULD BE IF YOUR MARRIAGE SO FAR WERE A 10-GAME SEASON.

> ❯ ASK YOUR PARENT OR CHILD

"Well done, my good and faithful servant. You have been faithful in handling this small amount, so now I will give you many more responsibilities."
—Matthew 25:23

19

WHAT YOUR RECORD WOULD BE IN TERMS OF YOUR SUPPORT OF THE FAMILY.

❯ ASK YOUR FRIEND WHAT YOUR RECORD WOULD BE IN TERMS OF SUPPORTING HIM OR HER AS A FRIEND.

Session 2

WHAT IS STRENGTH?

Recognizing the Real Strength God Has Given You

WHAT EACH PERSON WILL NEED:

- ❯ Bible
- ❯ Pen
- ❯ A sheet of paper, a slice of bread, or a phone book
- ❯ *Quiet Strength: Men's Bible Study* guide

THINK ABOUT IT

(15 minutes)

 There are two common yet different types of men. The first are the men who are strong, steely, and unemotional. They hold their ground and stand through the storm. The second are the supportive and sensitive men. They are aware of the needs of others and are able to be there for the ones they love. The problem with the first

Coach Dungy constantly reminded his players of the following mindset he expected and lived:
"Whatever It Takes
No Excuses,
No Explanations"
How would the Church be different if Christians adopted the same mindset regarding their faith?

 When you see this icon, have someone in your group read the section aloud as others follow along.

Complete a quick check-in regarding the commitments you made at the end of the last session. Let each person share how he followed through.

type is that they can tend to be overbearing, opinionated, and selfish. The problem with the second is that they are sometimes passive, intimidated, and ineffective.

Is it possible that real strength is found in both? Is real strength—quiet strength—a mix of steely nerves and emotional intelligence? Can real strength be found in the man who is courageous enough to weather the storms of life and humble enough to look for support?

Perhaps real strength isn't found in a personality type or even an outlook on life. Regardless of how we are wired, strength is found in having the faith to look to God to change us and to obey Him in what He has called each of us to do.

Think about the people you have met whom you consider to be strong men or women. List their names below, then write the reasons you think each person is strong next to his or her name.

Who	Why

With a partner, discuss the following:

- ❯ Share a story about one of the people you listed that demonstrates that person's strength.

- ❯ Who are some historical figures or celebrities you would consider to be strong? What makes each of them strong?

- ❯ How does society define strength?

- ❯ How do you define strength?

- ❯ Under which definition do the people on your list fall? What about the historical figures or celebrities?

- ❯ What are some common myths or misperceptions about strength?

TALK ABOUT IT *(20 minutes)*

Coach Dungy has been criticized because he doesn't often yell at his players, intimidate them, or get in their faces. A lot of people just don't think you can effectively coach without those tactics. But Coach Dungy believes that strength isn't found in being loud, aggressive, or in-your-face; strength is found, instead, in his integrity, determination, and consistency.

Strength is inside *him, and it is inside* you. *It is revealed when your relationships get difficult and you want to just walk away. It shows itself when your commitments are no longer convenient or comfortable. Strength is made evident when you hear God calling you*

23

out of the old way and into the new—and you follow that call. Real strength is found in reaching up to God in the middle of uncertainty and fear while standing in faith on the promises He has given.

If you haven't recognized the *real* strength that God has given you, it's likely that you are comparing yourself to a standard that God has not called you to—a worldly idea of strength. Take a moment to think about a time in your life when you exhibited *real* strength—the kind of strength defined above, the kind of quiet strength of Coach Dungy. Find a partner, and tell him the story you thought of. Then discuss:

> *"Tony Dungy is the first African-American coach to ever win the Super Bowl. That, in itself, is a great honor, but interestingly enough he is a man who has used his position of notoriety to behave in a quiet and strong way in the face of personal tragedy and he has influenced a lot of his fellow citizens."*
> —President George W. Bush

❯ WERE YOU SURPRISED BY YOUR ACTIONS? WHY OR WHY NOT?

❯ WHAT MOTIVATED YOU TO SHOW STRENGTH IN THAT SITUATION?

❯ TELL ABOUT A TIME WHEN YOU EXHIBITED WEAKNESS.

❯ WHAT WAS THE DIFFERENCE IN THE EMOTIONS, CIRCUMSTANCES, AND OUTCOMES OF THE TWO EVENTS?

USELESS TRIVIA

 Since the beginning of the World's Strongest Man event in 1977 to the most recent 2006 competition, four Americans have won. Can you name any of them? (See page 71 for the answer.)

STUDY IT *(20 minutes)*

During his first year playing for the Pittsburgh Steelers, Coach Dungy studied the book of Nehemiah. That study gave Coach Dungy the strength he needed through many of his struggles in the NFL. He explains three main points that he carried with him from the book of Nehemiah:

"First, Nehemiah's opportunity came in God's time, not his own. Second, Nehemiah diligently prepared his mind and his heart so he would be ready when God's time arrived. Third, Nehemiah needed to be prepared to take on the problems, doubt, and adversity that would come his way both from the outside or from within."

> *"Each time he said, 'My grace is all you need. My power works best in weakness.' So now I am glad to boast about my weaknesses, so that the power of Christ can work through me. That's why I take pleasure in my weaknesses, and in the insults, hardships, persecutions, and troubles that I suffer for Christ. For when I am weak, then I am strong."*
> —2 Corinthians 12:9-11

The book of Nehemiah is packed with wisdom for attacking problems or circumstances that require strength we don't have on our own. Form groups of four or fewer. Read the first chapter of the book of Nehemiah, then discuss:

❯ **What are some of the ways Nehemiah exhibited strength in this passage?**

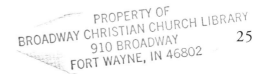

> ❯ Nehemiah started his work with prayer. Tell about a time when God gave you strength to do something you had to do.

Read Nehemiah 2:1-10.

> ❯ Why do you think Nehemiah was afraid when King Artaxerxes asked him why he looked sad?

> ❯ How did Nehemiah exhibit strength in this passage?

Read Nehemiah 2:11-20.

> ❯ How did Nehemiah exhibit strength in this passage?

> ❯ What parts did both God and Nehemiah play in the rebuilding of the wall?

> ❯ How would this account be different for Nehemiah if he didn't act in the strength God gave him? How would it be different for the Israelites?

> ❯ What situation are you facing that requires you to be strong in faith and action?

> ❯ How can the insights you've gained from Nehemiah's story help you as you face that situation?

USEFUL TRIVIA

As Nehemiah and the Israelites built the wall, Sanballat and Tobiah tried to lessen the Israelites' resolve by ridiculing them with some pretty sorry put-downs. What did Sanballat or Tobiah say? (See page 71 for the answer.)

LIVE IT *(10 minutes)*

Have at least one person in your group try a few of the following feats of strength. Don't give in to the temptation to skip this and just read it. Give at least one of these a try. And you can all try all of them if you wish.

- ❯ FOLD A SHEET OF PAPER IN HALF NINE TIMES.

- ❯ EAT A SLICE OF BREAD IN 30 SECONDS OR LESS. (THE BREAD MUST BE DRY, AND YOU CAN'T TAKE A DRINK OF ANYTHING.)

- ❯ TOUCH THE FLOOR WHILE KEEPING YOUR REAR AND HEELS AGAINST THE WALL.

- ❯ RIP AN ENTIRE PHONE BOOK IN HALF.

Discuss:

- ❯ WERE YOU SURPRISED BY THE RESULTS OR EFFORTS DURING ANY OF THESE FEATS OF STRENGTH?

- ❯ HOW WOULD THE RESULTS HAVE BEEN DIFFERENT IF YOU MADE THE FOLLOWING ADJUSTMENTS:

  - ❯ YOU CUT THE PAPER INSTEAD OF FOLDING IT?

  - ❯ YOU DRANK SOME MILK AS YOU ATE THE BREAD?

  - ❯ YOU HAD A FRIEND TO LEAN ON AS YOU TOUCHED THE FLOOR?

  - ❯ YOU RIPPED THE PHONE BOOK A FEW PAGES AT A TIME?

- ❯ HOW HAVE YOU SEEN GOD GIVE YOU THE STRENGTH TO MAKE DIFFICULT THINGS SIMPLE?

- How have you seen something simple become difficult because you failed to involve God in the process?

- What specific area in your life do you need God's strength for right now?

- How might trusting God for this be a quality of "quiet strength"?

Form groups of three or fewer. Share your answers to the last two questions with your group. Pray for God's strength and help in the circumstances you shared.

COMMIT TO IT

Before you conclude this session, choose to complete one of the action points that follow or another action point you come up with. Commit to completing the action point before your next meeting, and be prepared to share what happened or what you learned.

Option 1: Read chapters 4-9 of Tony Dungy's *Quiet Strength*. Make a list of the characteristics you see in Coach Dungy that exhibit quiet strength.

Option 2: If you are struggling in an area of your life that you can't seem to conquer on your own, talk privately with a Christian friend. Ask him for support, counsel, and consistent prayer. Invite him to check in on your progress through the next several months.

Option 3: Read the rest of the book of Nehemiah. Look for the ways Nehemiah showed real strength.

Session 3

WHAT IS SUCCESS?

Defining Yourself Beyond What You Do

> **WHAT EACH PERSON WILL NEED:**
> ❯ Bible
> ❯ Pen
> ❯ *Quiet Strength: Men's Bible Study* guide

THINK ABOUT IT *(20 minutes)*

 God has given us the desire and ability to achieve. We're created to build, develop, and strive. There is something inside all of us that wants our lives to matter—to make real impact in our jobs, relationships, and world. And tasting success gives us the courage and confidence to go after greater things. Think for a moment about your accomplishments thus far. What are you most proud of? Did you launch a new initiative on the job? Did God use you to build a faith-filled home? Maybe you're proud

> *Complete a quick check-in regarding the commitments you made at the end of the last session. Let each person share how he followed through.*

> **When you see this icon, have someone in your group read the section aloud as others follow along.**

29

of your kids, the building project at church, or finishing school.

Make a quick list right now of some of your accomplishments. Don't be afraid of bragging. It's important to see where you've been as you try to move forward.

Now share with the rest of the group an accomplishment in your life that you are proud of. Explain why you're proud of that accomplishment. Make sure everyone has a chance to share.

 Coach Dungy's life is a litany of accomplishment. Before coaching, he was a defensive back with the Super Bowl champion Pittsburgh Steelers. The professional teams he has led have won nearly twice as many games as they have lost. He led the Colts to a Super Bowl victory in 2007 and to four other playoff

The goal of this study is not to plow through all of the questions and content. The goal is to grow closer to Jesus, grow closer to each other, and be changed by God. Don't be afraid to stop, dig deeper, or pray for one another during this session. Keep your eyes open for teachable moments that God brings to your group, and respond accordingly.

appearances before that. He was named Coach of the Year in 2005. Coach Dungy is the picture of success. He is obviously a gifted leader, strategist, and motivator. He knows what it takes. But you might be a little surprised at how Coach Dungy defines success—take a look:

"God gives each one of us unique gifts, abilities, and passions. How well we use those qualities to have an impact on the world around us determines how 'successful' we really are."

There's nothing there about winning, about overcoming, about positions held, or even accomplishments. Just impacting the world. Discuss the following:

❯ DO YOU AGREE WITH COACH DUNGY'S DEFINITION OF SUCCESS? WHY OR WHY NOT?

❯ WOULD YOU SAY YOUR GREATEST ACCOMPLISHMENT IN LIFE THUS FAR IS A SUCCESS ACCORDING TO COACH DUNGY'S DEFINITION? EXPLAIN.

❯ WHAT IS A SIGNIFICANT FAILURE YOU'VE HAD?

❯ HOW DOES COACH DUNGY'S DEFINITION OF SUCCESS APPLY TO THAT FAILURE?

TALK ABOUT IT *(10 minutes)*

Success is often defined and recognized in terms of what we do. Most bosses, coaches, and customers aren't so concerned about who we are. They are interested in results. Most of us have yet to hear a boss say, "You lost the account, but you're a swell guy. How about a promotion?" Even our friends and loved ones often measure us on how we perform and act in the relationship. There is tremendous pressure on every man (and boy) to produce. We are "wired" to perform and strive for results. That wiring often leads to some very positive results in our lives.

However, as most employees, businessmen, or students would attest, our success is usually based on our most recent performance. Our successes are soon forgotten as those who evaluate us (including ourselves) ask, "What's next?"

> "My purpose in life is simply to glorify God. We have to be careful that we don't let the pursuit of our life's goals, no matter how important they seem, cause us to lose sight of our purpose."
> —*Tony Dungy*

Coach Dungy's definition points to a refreshing idea about success. If success is about making the most of our potential, success is tied much more to who we are. *It is what we do with what* we have *that determines our success. Results are important, but not necessarily the most accurate gauge of our success.*

Try this exercise to bring the point home. Get in groups of three or fewer. Have each man tell the others who he is *without* mentioning anything he has done. Tell the group who you are and what you're about without sharing any of the jobs you've done, volunteer work you've completed, committees you've been on, projects you've completed, or anything else you've accomplished or done.

After everyone takes a turn, discuss:

❯ HOW IS THE DESCRIPTION YOU GAVE OF YOURSELF DIFFERENT OR SIMILAR TO THE WAY YOU USUALLY INTRODUCE YOURSELF OR DESCRIBE YOURSELF TO THE PEOPLE YOU MEET?

❯ WHY DO YOU THINK MEN OFTEN DEFINE THEMSELVES BY WHAT THEY DO?

❯ WHO ARE PEOPLE YOU KNOW OR KNOW ABOUT WHO MEET THE COACH'S DEFINITION OF SUCCESS? EXPLAIN.

❯ WHAT NEEDS TO CHANGE IN YOUR LIFE FOR YOU TO BECOME MORE SUCCESSFUL IN *WHO YOU ARE*?

USELESS TRIVIA

It's an accomplishment just to get the Super Bowl. But four coaches have gone and lost four times. Name at least two of them. (See page 72 for answers.)

STUDY IT *(30 minutes)*

 God is the only one who has a complete perspective of where we've been, where we are, and where we are going. God knows exactly what matters on this earth, the real impact of our lives, and exactly how we will be measured when we move on to eternity. Fortunately, God has shared the key details with us in Scripture. God defines our success, and He has clearly demonstrated what it takes for us to truly be successful.

With a partner, answer the following questions about each passage:

❯ WHAT DOES THIS PASSAGE SAY ABOUT SUCCESS?

❯ HOW IS THAT SIMILAR TO OR DIFFERENT FROM HOW MOST
PEOPLE LOOK AT SUCCESS?

Psalm 1:1-3

_____
_____
_____
_____
_____
_____
_____

1 Samuel 16:7

_____
_____
_____
_____
_____
_____
_____

Micah 6:6-8

_____
_____
_____
_____
_____
_____
_____

Matthew 22:34-40

_____

_____

_____

_____

_____

_____

After about 10 minutes, come back together and discuss:

❯ WHAT SURPRISES OR INSIGHTS DID YOU HAVE AS YOU LOOKED AT THESE PASSAGES?

❯ HOW IS GOD'S DEFINITION OF SUCCESS DIFFERENT FROM HOW MOST PEOPLE DEFINE IT?

In Acts 7, Stephen gave a sort of sermon after being arrested by the Jewish leaders. Stephen gave a summary of Jewish history and how it all culminated in Jesus, and he rebuked the religious leaders.
Read Acts 7:54-60 to see how his sermon was received.

The earthly results wouldn't point us to think of Stephen's efforts as the most successful sermon. No one came to Christ as far as we can tell. His listeners didn't appear to grow closer to God. When your audience shakes their fists, plugs their ears, and yells at you, it's likely your message is not being well received. And martyrdom is a nearly certain sign that your speech didn't resonate with your listeners. But verses 55-56 show us that Stephen looked

to heaven and saw God's glory and Jesus Himself when he finished.
It appears that God was pleased with Stephen's efforts. And his
efforts must have had a lasting impact on Saul, who witnessed and
approved of Stephen's death. Is it possible that Stephen's story shows
us that real and lasting success is found first in loving God and then
in obeying Him?

Discuss:

> ❯ WHAT ELSE DOES STEPHEN'S STORY TEACH US ABOUT SUCCESS?

Form groups of four or fewer. Work together to create a
definition of success. Start with the Scriptures you studied. You can
also incorporate Coach Dungy's thoughts and your own thoughts.
Once your group has settled on or come close to a definition, write
it in the space below. Then think about whether you are willing
to allow that definition to define success for you. If not, make the
appropriate adjustments, and write down the definition that you
want to use as a guide for success in your life.

The group's definition of success

_____

_____

_____

_____

My guiding definition of success

_____

_____

_____

_____

In your group, discuss:

○ Do you think Stephen was a success? Why or why not?

○ Stephen's experience emphasizes loving God and then obeying God as the ultimate success. Do you agree? Why or why not?

○ How does your group's definition incorporate loving God? obeying God?

○ If loving and obeying God are key components of success, how would you say you're doing?

USEFUL TRIVIA

The Bible clearly states that there were at least five people who were martyred for their faith. How many can you name? (See page 72 for the answers.)

LIVE IT *(15 minutes)*

Many men find and define success in their work. And work is a very important part of who we are. However, our jobs are just one part of our lives. It's important to consider all areas of our lives as we evaluate our success.

Use the definition you wrote for success on page 36 to consider how successful you are in each of the following areas:

Family

STRUGGLING 1 2 3 4 5 6 7 8 9 10 SUCCEEDING

_____

_____

Faith

STRUGGLING 1 2 3 4 5 6 7 8 9 10 SUCCEEDING

_____

_____

Friends

STRUGGLING 1 2 3 4 5 6 7 8 9 10 SUCCEEDING

_____

_____

Ministry/service

STRUGGLING 1 2 3 4 5 6 7 8 9 10 SUCCEEDING

_____

_____

Other

STRUGGLING 1 2 3 4 5 6 7 8 9 10 SUCCEEDING

_____

_____

Find a partner to discuss:

❯ AS YOU LOOK AT THIS LIST, WHAT SEEMS TO BE WORKING?
   WHAT NEEDS ATTENTION?

❯ How does your life need to change to find success as you've defined it?

❯ What are the first steps you'll take to begin implementing that change?

Choose one of the areas listed above that needs to see change. Explain to your partner what you need from God. Then pray together for God's help.

COMMIT TO IT

Before you conclude this session, choose to complete one of the action points that follow or another action point you come up with:

OPTION 1: Read chapters 10-12 of Tony Dungy's *Quiet Strength*. Look for experiences that match the Coach's definition of success. Make a note of how those experiences opened the doors for future success.

OPTION 2: One important aspect of success is letting go of goals, expectations, or activities that distract us from what really matters. Ask God to show you one thing in your life that is getting in the way of His definition of success for you. Then let that thing go.

OPTION 3: Ask God to show you one area of your life that needs a new definition of success. Share your definition of success (on page 36) with someone who is closely connected with that area, and ask him or her how you can move toward your definition of success. You could talk with your spouse about your marriage, your pastor about ministry areas, or a friend at work about your job.

WHAT IS YOUR SECURITY?

Building a Rock-Solid Foundation

THINK ABOUT IT *(10 minutes)*

More than 13 years ago, Bryan Berg secured a world record by building a house of cards that was over 25 feet high. He didn't use adhesives or cut notches. Balance and the weight of the cards kept his house intact. Some time later, Bryan built the largest playing card structure—a 14-cubic-foot model of Cinderella's castle complete with turrets and tunnels. If you've ever built a house of cards, you know that a slight gust or bump brings the whole house down.

Life is often like a house of cards. There are a few cards at the bottom that just about everything rests on. An unexpected wind of change at work and the mortgage, car payment, and an entire way of life could collapse. A strong

> *Complete a quick check-in regarding the commitments you made at the end of the last session. Let each person share how he followed through.*

nudge on a family member's health and the daily routine falls into a tumult. Change is sure to come, and there's no guarantee that it will be pleasant.

Take a moment to think about the foundational areas of your life that are supporting the other aspects of how you live. Try to think of four "foundations" that have the potential to drastically change things for you. Write each of those foundations in one of the four bottom cards that follow. Then list some of the important things in your life that are dependent on those foundations. You could write "my job" on one of the bottom cards, and "my home," "food," and "future opportunities" on the cards it supports.

With a partner, discuss:

- ❯ WHAT FOUR FOUNDATIONS DID YOU LIST?

- ❯ WHAT WOULD HAPPEN IF ANY OF THESE FOUNDATIONS COLLAPSED?

- ❯ ON A SCALE OF 1-5 WHERE 1 IS "NO WORRIES" AND 5 IS "COMPLETELY FREAKED OUT," HOW WOULD YOU RATE YOUR CURRENT SENSE OF SECURITY IN EACH OF THOSE AREAS? EXPLAIN.

TALK ABOUT IT *(20 minutes)*

It's happened to most of us—the day we realized life would never be the same. The loss of a child, a layoff, an accident, a health problem, divorce, or another event that changed everything. Maybe you saw it coming, maybe you should have, or maybe it just happened. Regardless, it happened and you realized that the ground you had been standing on was crumbling beneath you. And you still sometimes wonder if you've fully recovered.

Coach Dungy describes his day like this: "My real and painful experience of being fired was an all-too-common part of the human condition in the young 21st century. I reminded myself that it was temporary.... But my emotions were a mixture of peace and bewilderment with a swirl of unanswered questions. What's next? What could we have done differently?

"I kept reminding myself that I would move on, that things would turn out all right professionally, that Lauren and the children were resilient enough to handle all of this.

"When will I hear your voice Lord? Soon, I hope.

"I knew everything would ultimately be fine, but at the moment—on that rain-swept night of January 14, 2002—my Explorer and my spirits traveled under the same dark clouds."

> *"I think there are times when I believe God welcomes the circus into our lives to give us an opportunity to show that there's another way to live and respond to things."*
> —Tony Dungy

Discuss with a partner:

❯ HAVE YOU EVER EXPERIENCED AN EVENT THAT CHANGED EVERYTHING FOR YOU?

❯ HOW HAS THAT EXPERIENCE SHAPED YOU?

❯ TO WHAT DEGREE HAVE YOU RECOVERED OR ADAPTED TO THE EXPERIENCE?

 No one can completely understand the pain you've faced. But Coach Dungy shares some profound insights on dealing with personal loss in Quiet Strength *that you may find helpful:*

"For me, focusing on the things I knew to be true helped me find the path."

> *It is possible that you or your partner may bring up some experiences that still have a lot of emotion connected to them. You don't have to try to "fix" each other or pretend everything is OK. Rather, just be there for each other and look together to God for His healing.*

Discuss:

❯ WHAT DO YOU KNOW TO BE TRUE THAT YOU CAN FOCUS ON
AS YOU LIVE THROUGH THE EFFECTS OF YOUR LIFE-CHANGING
EVENT?

❯ READ 1 CORINTHIANS 12:9 AND ROMANS 5:3-6. HOW DO THESE
PASSAGES APPLY TO YOUR CIRCUMSTANCES?

❯ HOW CAN THE MEN IN THIS GROUP SUPPORT YOU IN THIS?

Ask your partner how you can pray for him. Then spend about five minutes lifting each other up in prayer.

USELESS TRIVIA

There's no such thing as job security for NFL coaches. But winning a Super Bowl doesn't hurt. Who was the youngest coach to lead his team to a victory in the Big Game? Hint: It was also his first year as the coach. (See page 73 for the answer.)

STUDY IT *(20 minutes)*

God has given you friends, family, and other resources to help you through life-changing events. It's important to lean on them when tough times come. But in the end, the only foundation that you can always lean on is God. God is the only unshakeable foundation on which we can build our lives.

It is the focus on God as Tony Dungy's foundation that brought him through pain and disappointment: "The pain . . .

will never go away. But in the midst of it all, I truly believe that hope is available to all *of us—for joy in today and peace in the certainty that heaven's glory awaits us."*

Form groups of four or fewer. With your group, look up the following passages. Discuss what you read, then record what truth each passage gives that you can focus on when life doesn't seem secure. Make sure to discuss the proof the passages give that God is a sure foundation for our lives.

TRUTH TO FOCUS ON:

❯ Psalm 91:1-6

TRUTH TO FOCUS ON:

❯ Hebrews 13:5-6

TRUTH TO FOCUS ON:

❯ Titus 3:4-7

Discuss:

❯ HOW HAVE YOU SEEN GOD'S FAITHFULNESS IN THE MIDST OF DIFFICULT CIRCUMSTANCES IN YOUR LIFE?

❯ IN YOUR MOST HONEST ASSESSMENT, HOW RELIANT ON GOD ARE YOU FOR YOUR FOUNDATION AND SECURITY?

❯ WHAT THINGS IN LIFE DO YOU RELY ON MORE THAN YOU SHOULD?

LIVE IT *(10 minutes)*

Take a moment to pray silently right now that God would show you the things in your life that you are relying too heavily on for your security. God may show you that you are putting undue faith in your job, in your skills, or in your intellect. Find something you have with you that represents what God has revealed to you. You could use a credit card to symbolize your reliance on money or your wedding ring to symbolize too much reliance on your spouse.

Hold that item tightly in your fist. Ask for God to help you to rely on Him first. Prayerfully give that area of your life to Christ. As you do, open your fist and let the item drop to the table or ground. Remain in an attitude of prayer until everyone has dropped his item.

Then have one person pray something like the following aloud: *Father, we thank You that we are Your children. Thank You that You are able and willing to protect and help us. Please take the hurts and disappointments we have encountered in our lives. Forgive us for looking to things on this earth for our foundation and security. As we give these things up to You, we pray that You would replace them with your presence, peace, and assurance. In Jesus' name, amen.*

COMMIT TO IT

Before you conclude this session, choose to complete one of the action points that follow or another action point you come up with.

Commit to completing the action point before your next meeting, and be prepared to share what happened or what you learned.

OPTION 1: Read chapter 18 of Tony Dungy's *Quiet Strength*. Highlight statements or sections that give encouragement for facing difficult times.

OPTION 2: Follow up on your commitment to look to God as your foundation. Take one small step that shows your trust in God instead of the other thing you've been looking to. For example, you might cut up one of your credit cards if you've been relying on money. You could spend the first five minutes of work in prayer if you've been relying on your job.

OPTION 3: Read Psalm 121 every day until your next meeting. Try to memorize it before your next meeting. Personalize the psalm by substituting your name for "you" and "Israel" as you read.

WHAT IS YOUR SIGNIFICANCE?

Finding Your Importance in Making a Difference

WHAT EACH PERSON WILL NEED:

- ❯ Bible
- ❯ Coffee (one cup for the whole group)
- ❯ Water (one cup for the whole group)
- ❯ Spoon or straw
- ❯ Pen
- ❯ *Quiet Strength: Men's Bible Study* guide

THINK ABOUT IT *(10 minutes)*

Think for a moment about the last significant purchase you made or a goal that you strove after and achieved. How long did it take until that possession or goal no longer brought the satisfaction it once gave you? How long did it take until you started looking for and striving toward something else?

Sooner or later, we all are forced to deal with the serious questions of significance. What really matters in life? How much is enough? What is my life for? What am I doing with what God has given me? What is God's plan for my life?

> *Complete a quick check-in regarding the commitments you made at the end of the last session. Let each person share how he followed through.*

Try this exercise to help you start thinking about what really matters. Use the space below to fill out your "to do" list for the day (or for the next day if today is nearly over). Just write down everything you plan or need to accomplish today. Put an "A" next to every item that is a top priority for the day, a "B" next to each item that is somewhat important, and a "C" next to the items that aren't at all pressing.

Now underline all of the items on your list that will impact your life one month from now. Circle each item that you think will be important to you five years from now. Put a star next to each item that you think will be significant in your life as you look back to today 10 years from now.

TO DO:

DATE:_____ TIME

Ⓐ <u>Worship Team practice</u> 7:00 ☑

○ _____ ☐

○ _____ ☐

○ _____ ☐

○ _____ ☐

○ _____ ☐

"When a game ends, win or lose, it's time to prepare for the next one. The coaches and players really don't have time to celebrate or to stay down, because Sunday's gone and Monday's here. And no matter what happened yesterday, you have to be ready to play next Sunday.

"That's how it works—just like life.

"It's the journey that matters. Learning is more important than the test."

—Tony Dungy

Discuss:

❯ WHAT INSIGHTS DID YOU HAVE DURING THIS EXERCISE?

❯ WHAT ARE THE MOST IMPORTANT THINGS IN YOUR LIFE
RIGHT NOW?

❯ HOW DO YOUR DAILY TASKS LEAD YOU TO OR AWAY FROM
FOCUSING ON THOSE THINGS?

❯ HOW DO YOU THINK YOUR PRIORITIES MIGHT CHANGE IN THE
NEXT 10 YEARS?

TALK ABOUT IT *(20 minutes)*

 The only work you can do that has eternal value is work with people. Possessions, organizations, companies, buildings—everything else—will one day fade away or burn up. But people are eternal. Real and lasting significance comes through the way you interact with and affect people. Who you are today is at least in part a result of how those closest to you loved you or failed to do so. When you interact with your friends, family, and coworkers, you are affecting eternity.

Think for a moment about your life in elementary school. Who had the most positive influence on you during that time of your life? With a partner share how that person impacted you.

Now think about a person who positively influenced you during junior high or high school. Find a new partner, and tell him how that person had an effect on you. Find another new partner, and tell him how a different person had a positive impact on you during your adult years.

Then discuss:

> ❯ WHAT HAVE THE THREE PEOPLE YOU TALKED ABOUT "DEPOSITED" IN YOU THAT YOU STILL CARRY TODAY?

> ❯ HOW WOULD YOUR LIFE BE DIFFERENT IF THOSE PEOPLE REFUSED OR NEGLECTED TO GET INVOLVED IN YOUR LIFE?

> ❯ HOW HAVE YOU HAD A POSITIVE IMPACT ON SOMEONE'S LIFE? WHAT DID IT TAKE FOR YOU TO MAKE A DIFFERENCE?

"For no one can lay any foundation other than the one we already have—Jesus Christ. Anyone who builds on that foundation may use a variety of materials—gold, silver, jewels, wood, hay, or straw. But on the judgment day, fire will reveal what kind of work each builder has done. The fire will show if a person's work has any value."
—1 Corinthians 3:11-13

USELESS TRIVIA

Most professional and Olympic athletes have pretty short careers. A number of athletes make significant contributions surprisingly late in life. How many of these "oldest" sports figures can you name? Who was the oldest athlete to:

    a. score 50 points in one NBA game?
    b. hold a heavyweight boxing title?
    c. win a Super Bowl as the quarterback?
    d. win the Heisman Trophy?

(See page 73 for the answers.)

STUDY IT *(25 minutes)*

There is a trap before every man. It begins with the words "When I" and ends with "then." "<u>When I</u> get this promotion, <u>then</u> I'll start giving tithes and offerings to God." "<u>When I</u> move, <u>then</u> I'll start reaching out to my neighbors." It's an effective trap because the hope behind it is sincere and the results are powerfully motivating. "<u>When I</u> retire, <u>then</u> I'll become a missionary."

Perhaps you will one day move into full-time ministry or be freed up to do more for God. But if you hope to be effective at all, you had better make the most of what God has put before you right now. The wonderfully liberating truth is that you can live significantly <u>today</u>—no matter where you are or what you are doing. Since true significance is found in making a difference in the lives of people—and helping them know and grow in Jesus— it's not difficult to live significantly today. We simply need to get beyond the "When I, then" trap or the other excuses

"When (the Bucs owners) fired me, I was terribly disappointed that I wouldn't be able to stay the course with the organization we had built in Tampa. But I also recognized that I wasn't dealing with life-and-death issues. It wasn't as if I were helping women through high-risk pregnancies or helping people through physical problems, as my siblings were. They had what I considered to be critical jobs; I have never viewed my job as that important."
—Coach Dungy, reflecting on significance and being fired from the head coaching job at Tampa Bay

53

that get in our way from making a difference now. Let's explore this together.

Read Mark 10:17-31 together. Then work through the following exercises in groups of three or four. Discuss each question, and write down your thoughts as you talk with your group.

❯ IN VERSE 19, JESUS LISTS SIX OF THE TEN COMMANDMENTS. WHAT DO THE COMMANDMENTS HE LISTED HAVE IN COMMON, AND WHY DO YOU THINK JESUS CHOSE THESE COMMANDMENTS?

❯ WHAT IS THE "ONE THING" THAT THE RICH YOUNG MAN LACKED (VERSE 21)? WHY DO YOU SUPPOSE THIS WAS A PROBLEM FOR THAT MAN?

❯ WHAT DOES THE RICH YOUNG MAN'S RESPONSE IN VERSE 22 HAVE TO DO WITH SIGNIFICANCE?

❯ WHAT DO YOU THINK THIS ACCOUNT REVEALS ABOUT WHAT GOD VALUES? WHAT DOES VERSE 31 SAY ABOUT SIGNIFICANCE?

If Jesus were to tell you that you "lacked one thing," what would it be?

Spend a few moments asking God to show you, then fill in the sentence below. When you're done, share what you discovered with your group.

_____,
YOUR NAME

you lack only one thing: go and _____

_____
WHAT GOD IS CALLING YOU AWAY FROM.

Then come follow me.

With a partner, discuss:

❯ WHAT IS GETTING IN YOUR WAY OF LIVING A TRULY SIGNIFICANT
LIFE WHERE YOU ARE AT RIGHT NOW?

❯ HOW WOULD YOUR LIFE BE DIFFERENT IF YOU DID EXACTLY
WHAT YOU WROTE IN THE BLANKS ABOVE?

❯ WHAT DOES SIGNIFICANCE LOOK LIKE IN YOUR LIFE?

USEFUL TRIVIA

The Westminster Shorter Catechism gives an answer to the following question that various Christian denominations embrace. What is the answer it gives to this question: "What is the chief end of man?" (See page 74 for the answer.)

LIVE IT *(10 minutes)*

Put a glass of clear water in front of the group. Have someone in your group pour a spoonful or straw full of coffee into the water. Let it settle, then stir the water.

Discuss:

❯ WHAT IMPACT DID THE COFFEE HAVE ON THE WATER?

❯ HOW IS THAT SIMILAR TO OR DIFFERENT FROM THE IMPACT A MAN CAN HAVE ON THOSE WHO ARE CLOSEST TO HIM?

> *"And what do you benefit if you gain the whole world but lose your own soul? Is anything worth more than your soul?"*
> —Matthew 16:26

❯ HOW HAVE SMALL WORDS YOU'VE SPOKEN OR SMALL ACTIONS YOU'VE DONE HAD A LARGE IMPACT ON THOSE YOU LOVE?

❯ HOW CAN YOU MAKE AN IMPACT FOR GOD'S KINGDOM TODAY?

We all want significance. The truth is that it doesn't take much effort at all to have a profound impact on a life. A small careless word from a father can shake a child to the core. An insignificant act of kindness toward a coworker can change his or her outlook on the day—and even give him or her the confidence needed for joy and success. Your interactions with your coworkers, your family, and your friends may seem mundane. But your words can give confidence, hope, joy, peace, and can even point the way to salvation in Christ Jesus.

Prayerfully consider the people that God has in your life right now. Use the following space to list the people whom you think God may be calling you to impact. You might want to include family relationships God wants you to focus on, friends, neighbors, and coworkers. Next to each name, write down how you hope to impact that person's life.

PEOPLE IN MY LIFE   IMPACT I HOPE TO HAVE
_____   _____
_____   _____
_____   _____
_____   _____
_____   _____

Circle one of the relationships you'd like to focus on. Then find a partner, and pray together about how you can have a significant impact in that person's life.

COMMIT TO IT

Before you conclude this session, choose to complete one of the action points that follow or another action point you come up with. Commit to completing the action point before your next meeting, and be prepared to share what happened or what you learned.

OPTION 1: Read chapters 13-17 of Tony Dungy's *Quiet Strength.* Pay special attention to where Coach Dungy looks for significance in his life.

> *"Chuck Noll always reminded us that 'Football is what you are doing right now, but it's not your life's work. You've got to continue to prepare for your life's work.' "*
> —*Tony Dungy*

Option 2: If you have a significant relationship that doesn't seem quite right, take a risk that could have a lasting impact. Tell that person about this study, and humbly ask what it would take for you to have a more positive impact on his or her life. Avoid the temptation to defend yourself or ask anything in return. Rather, commit to making a difference in the way you interact.

Option 3: Identify one person you know who is not a Christian. Instead of making that person a project, become that person's friend. Pray for him or her regularly, and wait for the natural opportunities that God brings to talk about spiritual things. Take the first step toward building a friendship with that person before this group meets again.

Session 6

WHAT IS YOUR LEGACY?

Evaluating and Building the Story You'll Leave Behind

> ## WHAT EACH PERSON WILL NEED:
> ❯ Bible
> ❯ Pen
> ❯ *Quiet Strength: Men's Bible Study* guide

THINK ABOUT IT *(15 minutes)*

The Bible gives very little detail about a man named Enoch. We can read about his lineage in various passages; and the book of Jude tells us that Enoch gave a prophecy about God's judgment. But Enoch is best remembered for one simple sentence in Genesis 5:24: "Enoch walked with God; then he was no more, because God took him away" (NIV).

Enoch's remembrance is short, simple—and powerful. Enoch walked with God. This simple sentence says so much because we know what's behind "walking with God." We are well aware of the striving, discipline, obedience, and love for others that come with walking with God. We

> Complete a quick check-in regarding the commitments you made at the end of the last session. Let each person share how he followed through.

61

understand the sacrifice and joy surrounding an intimate friendship with our Creator. What more could a man want or aspire to be? What greater legacy could a person leave?

Imagine for a moment that God is going to write a one-sentence summary of your life similar to the summary He gave us of Enoch in His Word. In the space below, write down what you think God would write based on your life thus far. Then write down what you hope that summary would say at the end of your life.

SUMMARY OF LIFE SO FAR:

_____

_____

_____

_____

_____

_____

_____

SUMMARY I HOPE FOR:

_____

_____

_____

_____

_____

_____

_____

With a partner, discuss the following:

- SHARE YOUR TWO STATEMENTS, AND EXPLAIN HOW AND WHY THEY ARE DIFFERENT.

- ❯ IF YOU DIED TODAY, HOW SATISFIED WOULD YOU BE OF THE LEGACY YOU HAVE LEFT?

- ❯ WHAT DO YOU WANT TO ACCOMPLISH BEFORE YOU DIE?

"I love coaching football, and winning a Super Bowl was a goal I've had for a long time. But it has never been my purpose in life."
—Tony Dungy

TALK ABOUT IT

(20 minutes)

 Coach Dungy is leaving a God-honoring legacy. He has broken down barriers for African-American coaches. He used the platform of a Super Bowl victory to bring glory to Jesus Christ. More importantly, he has put his family first and has set an example of quiet strength in the way he coaches. Coach Dungy clearly explains that who he is, what he believes, and how he lives is a part of the legacy his parents passed down to him.

Coach Dungy describes a part of his father's legacy. Early on in life, his father taught him to respond rather than react—to always look at how he could make the situation better. He shares the following exchange he had with his father after he received a technical foul during a basketball game:

"Venting," I called it.

"Dumb," my dad called it. Our exchanges usually ran something like this:

"Did you change the referee's call?"

"No."

"Did it make the situation better?"

"No, but I felt better, and then I could focus."

"Well, you might have felt better faster if you were thinking about the next play instead of taking three or four or ten plays to 'vent.' You waste a lot of emotion and energy in venting or in worrying about an injustice or something you can't do anything about."

The legacy lives on in Coach Dungy today. When he encounters injustice, difficulty, or opposition, his natural approach is to look at how he can use his energy effectively.

> *"That's what this is all about. Touching lives. Building a legacy— not necessarily on the field but in those places that most people will never see. Trying to be faithful in the position God has given me."*
> —*Tony Dungy*

Your father has left a legacy that you carry with you or that you must overcome. Think for a moment about three things that your father has left or instilled in you. You can list physical characteristics, emotional traits, or spiritual traits. They can be positive or negative, but try to think of the things that stick with you the most. Write them below.

_____

_____

_____

_____

_____

_____

Now find one thing in the room that symbolizes and summarizes the legacy your father gave you. You could point to food in the room because your father taught you to provide for your family without complaining. You could point to an unstable chair because your father was absent and you had to fight insecurity as a result.

Find a partner, and explain the item you chose. After each person has shared, discuss:

❯ WHAT PART OF YOUR FATHER'S LEGACY DO YOU WANT TO EMULATE?

❯ WHAT PART DO YOU WANT TO OVERCOME?

❯ HOW HAS THE LEGACY YOUR FATHER LEFT TO YOU MADE IT MORE DIFFICULT OR EASY FOR YOU TO LEAVE A POSITIVE LEGACY?

❯ AS COACH DUNGY WOULD ASK, WHAT ARE YOU GOING TO DO TO MAKE THE SITUATION BETTER?

USELESS TRIVIA

Nearly all professional coaches have tasted success at some level. But there are a few who build sports legacies. How many of these sports "legends" can you identify?

a. Which NHL coach has led his teams to take 9 Stanley Cup trophies?

b. Which Major League manager has won more games than any other?

c. Which coach has won the most NBA playoff games?

(See page 74 for the answers.)

STUDY IT *(20 minutes)*

If there's one idea that you should have picked up by now in these six studies, it's that you matter. You matter to God. You matter to those around you. What you do matters. What you leave undone matters. For better or worse, you are leaving a legacy. Whether you like it or not, the world—and especially those around you—is affected by the way you act, the things you say, and the things you do.

Form groups of four or fewer. Read Matthew 25:31-46, then discuss:

❯ WHAT ARE THE DIFFERENCES BETWEEN THE SHEEP AND THE GOATS IN THIS PASSAGE?

❯ WHICH OF THE THINGS IN VERSES 35-36 HAVE YOU DONE?

❯ WHAT ARE SOME OF THE OTHER THINGS YOU OR OTHERS YOU KNOW HAVE DONE THAT COULD BE INCLUDED IN THE LIST IN VERSES 35-36?

❯ WHAT DO VERSES 40 AND 45 SAY ABOUT THE IMPACT OF YOUR ACTIONS?

❯ WHAT DOES THIS PASSAGE SAY ABOUT THE LEGACY YOU'RE BUILDING?

❯ WHAT DOES THIS PASSAGE MOTIVATE YOU TO DO DIFFERENTLY WITH THE REMAINING YEARS OF YOUR LIFE?

Notice that in this passage, the sheep and goats were not surprised at which group they ended up in. Instead, they were surprised at Jesus' reaction to how they lived. They were deemed righteous or wicked in the way they approached Jesus. If you want to live a legacy that really lasts, if you want to make a real difference in this world, if you want to be counted with the righteous at the Final Judgment, you must rely on Jesus. If you fully give your life to Jesus, tremendous, world-changing works will flow out of your life, and you will share in the eternal reward and celebration of your legacy.

> *"And if you give even a cup of cold water to one of the least of my followers, you will surely be rewarded."*
> —Matthew 10:42

Spend a few minutes in silent prayer. Take a moment right now to think about where you stand before Jesus. If you have never turned control of your life over to Jesus or claimed Him as your Lord, take this opportunity to do so. If there are parts of your life that you are holding back from Jesus, give them over to Him during this time.

USEFUL TRIVIA

 Jesus' 12 disciples built on Christ's legacy and changed the world. Can you name the original 12 disciples? (See page 74 for the answer.)

LIVE IT *(10 minutes)*

 You may have been handed a lousy legacy, and you may not be too happy with the legacy you're currently building. The great news is that it's never too late to change your legacy. You can start leaving a positive and powerful legacy this very moment. Go through the following exercise to get started.

Create a sort of living will right now that centers on your legacy. Think about the legacy you want to leave to your family, those you know, and the world you live in. Fill in the blanks below with the names God brings to mind, then write down the legacy you hope to leave for each person.

To my family member(s) _____, I will leave you _____.

To my family member(s) _____, I will leave you _____.

To my family member(s) _____, I will leave you

_____.

To my friend or acquaintance _____, I will leave you _____.

To my friend or acquaintance _____, I will leave you _____.

To my friend or acquaintance _____, I will leave you _____.

To this world, I will leave you _____.

Find a partner, and share the most important item on your list. Pray together that God will show you how to build the legacy you've committed to leaving. Then discuss these questions:

❷ HOW HAVE THE LAST SIX WEEKS HELPED YOU DEFINE YOUR LEGACY?

❷ WHAT DO YOU HOPE TO CARRY FORWARD FROM THIS SIX-WEEK STUDY?

COMMIT TO IT

Before you conclude this session, choose to complete one of the action points that follow or another action point you come up with.

OPTION 1: Finish reading Tony Dungy's *Quiet Strength*. Look for how the legacy Coach Dungy's parents left plays out in his life.

OPTION 2: Put your legacy statements on award certificate paper. Then present those certificates to each person you included. Explain the legacy you hope to leave that person and how you plan on doing it.

OPTION 3: Call your mom, dad, or another person who influenced your life. Thank that person for the legacy he or she gave. Explain how that person's influence is lived out in your life today.

CONTACT

Name	Phone	E-mail
Name	Phone	E-mail
Name	Phone	E-mail
Name	Phone	E-mail
Name	Phone	E-mail
Name	Phone	E-mail
Name	Phone	E-mail
Name	Phone	E-mail
Name	Phone	E-mail
Name	Phone	E-mail
Name	Phone	E-mail
Name	Phone	E-mail
Name	Phone	E-mail
Name	Phone	E-mail
Name	Phone	E-mail
Name	Phone	E-mail
Name	Phone	E-mail
Name	Phone	E-mail
Name	Phone	E-mail
Name	Phone	E-mail
Name	Phone	E-mail
Name	Phone	E-mail
Name	Phone	E-mail
Name	Phone	E-mail
Name	Phone	E-mail
Name	Phone	E-mail
Name	Phone	E-mail
Name	Phone	E-mail

SESSION 1 USELESS TRIVIA ANSWER

1982 saw 9 games and 1987 saw 15 games due to player strikes.

SESSION 1 USEFUL TRIVIA ANSWER

The Bible doesn't say Saul's name *changed* to Paul. Acts 13:9 says that Saul was also called Paul. Paul was the Graeco-Roman form of the Jewish name Saul. Perhaps Saul started using the gentile form of his name as he ministered to the gentile people.

SESSION 2 USELESS TRIVIA ANSWERS

1. Bruce Wilhelm (1977, 1978)
2. Don Reinhoudt (1979)
3. Bill Kazmaier (1980, 1981, 1982)
4. Phil Pfister (2006)

SESSION 2 USEFUL TRIVIA ANSWERS

Sanballat gave three put-downs in Nehemiah 4:2:

1. What does this bunch of poor, feeble Jews think they're doing?
2. Do they think they can build the wall in a single day by just offering a few sacrifices?
3. Do they actually think they can make something of stones from a rubbish heap—and charred ones at that?

Tobiah gave the sorriest put-down in Nehemiah 4:3:

1. That stone wall would collapse if even a fox walked along the top of it!

Bud Grant was the first coach to lead a team to four Super Bowl defeats: the Minnesota Vikings. He was followed by Don Shula, Marv Levy, and Dan Reeves.

SESSION 3 USEFUL TRIVIA ANSWERS

The Bible gives evidence of the following martyrs. Other historical evidence shows that there were many more.

1. Zechariah was stoned to death (2 Chronicles 24:20-21).
2. Uriah was killed by King Jehoiakim (Jeremiah 26:23).
3. Stephen was stoned to death (Acts 7:59).
4. James the apostle was killed by King Herod (Acts 12:1-2).
5. Antipas from the church in Pergamum was put to death (Revelation 2:13).
6. Historical evidence shows that Paul was beheaded by Nero. Second Timothy 4:6 suggests that Paul was aware of his impending execution.
7. Historical evidence shows that Peter was crucified upside down by Nero. John 21:18-19 and 2 Peter 1:14 indicate that Peter was aware of his fate.
8. Hebrews 11:37 gives evidence that a number of prophets were

killed for their faith. Tradition tells us that Isaiah was sawed by Manasseh.

9. Revelation 11:7 points to the martyrdom of the two witnesses.

SESSION 4 USELESS TRIVIA ANSWER

Jon Gruden led the Tampa Bay Buccaneers to win Super Bowl XXVII at the age of 39 the year after Tony Dungy left the top spot.

SESSION 4 USEFUL TRIVIA ANSWERS

1. King David (he is associated with 73 of the psalms).
2. Asaph
3. The sons of Korah
4. Solomon
5. Moses
6. Heman (with the sons of Korah)
7. Ethan

SESSION 5 USELESS TRIVIA ANSWERS

a. Michael Jordan scored 51 points when he was 38.
b. George Foreman was 45 when he held the IBF and WBA heavyweight titles.
c. John Elway led the Denver Broncos to a Super Bowl victory when he was 38.
d. Florida State's Chris Weinke won the award when he was 28.

SESSION 5 USEFUL TRIVIA ANSWER

"The chief end of man is to glorify God and enjoy him forever."

SESSION 6 USELESS TRIVIA ANSWERS

a. Scotty Bowman

b. Connie Mack

c. Phil Jackson

SESSION 6 USEFUL TRIVIA ANSWER

1. Simon Peter

2. Andrew

3. John

4. James, the brother of John

5. Philip

6. Nathanael

7. Matthew (also called Levi)

8. Thaddaeus (also called Judas and Jude)

9. James the son of Alphaeus

10. Simon the Zealot

11. Thomas

12. Judas